Bibliographical Series
of Supplements to 'British Book News'
on Writers and Their Work

*

GENERAL EDITOR
Bonamy Dobrée

Writers and Their Work: No. 60

MATTHEW ARNOLD

by

KENNETH ALLOTT

PUBLISHED FOR
THE BRITISH COUNCIL
and the NATIONAL BOOK LEAGUE
by LONGMANS, GREEN & CO.

Two shillings net

Matthew Arnold (1822–88), a distinguished 'great Victorian' and a key-figure in poetry and criticism for the understanding of his age, is the subject of this perceptive essay by Mr. Kenneth Allott. Mr. Allott, who was educated at Durham University and St. Edmund Hall, Oxford, has published two collections of verse and is now a lecturer in English literature at Liverpool University. In recent years he has edited the poems of Habington and Praed, compiled an anthology of contemporary verse, and written a book on Graham Greene, but his chief interest is in Victorian literature. In the last two years he has edited a selection of Arnold's poems (Penguin Poets, 1954) and published *Five Uncollected Essays of Matthew Arnold* (1953); and he has just completed an anthology of Victorian prose on a new plan.

MATTHEW ARNOLD

a photograph taken in 1886

MATTHEW ARNOLD

by KENNETH ALLOTT

PUBLISHED FOR
THE BRITISH COUNCIL
and the NATIONAL BOOK LEAGUE
BY LONGMANS, GREEN & CO., LONDON, NEW YORK, TORONTO

LONGMANS, GREEN & CO. LTD.
6 & 7 Clifford Street, London W.1
Boston House, Strand Street, Cape Town
531 Little Collins Street, Melbourne

LONGMANS, GREEN & CO. INC.
55 Fifth Avenue, New York 3

LONGMANS, GREEN & CO.
20 Cranfield Road, Toronto 16

ORIENT LONGMANS LTD.
Calcutta Bombay Madras
Delhi Vijayawada Dacca

First published in 1955

Printed in Great Britain at The Curwen Press, Plaistow, E.13

CONTENTS

¶ MATTHEW ARNOLD was born at Laleham near Staines on 24 December 1822. He died at Liverpool on 15 April 1888, and is buried at Laleham.

MATTHEW ARNOLD

I

IF ANYONE asks what is central in Matthew Arnold's achievement—a question easily prompted by the volume of his work and the range of its interests—one of two replies is probable, in accordance with what is momentarily uppermost in our minds. It may be the missionary nature of Arnold's activities:

> Therefore to thee it was given
> Many to save with thyself

he wrote approvingly of his father, Dr. Thomas Arnold, in 'Rugby Chapel'—in which case we are likely to say that what is central, in the sense of being nearly omnipresent, is the moral and social passion which is the mainspring of such books as *Culture and Anarchy* and *Literature and Dogma*, and a sizable element in the poems and literary criticism. Alternatively, at a tangent to this, we may be thinking of what is distinctive, what most gives the taste of Arnold in Arnold's works, in which case we shall be found paying attention to a handful of poems and some selected pages of literary criticism which embody insights with an economical freshness and liveliness, and arguing that they are central in the sense that nobody else could have written them. In this manner a looseness in the original question brings forward two main aspects of Arnold's genius which cannot always be easily separated in his writings: on the one hand, the 'disinterestedness' with which objects, ideas and experiences may be viewed by him ('to see the object as in itself it really is')— the roll-call of examples includes such a poem as 'Growing Old', the splendid pages on the 'ways of handling nature' in *On the Study of Celtic Literature*, Arnold's opinion that the onlooker sees most of the game and that the critic should always remain a little remote from practice; on the other hand, the impulse to catechize and instruct, which involves him in judging ideas and even works of art partly by their relevance to apparent social needs—culture, Arnold insists, is a poor thing if it is self-regarding and, in a balanced view, •'moves by the force . . . of the moral and social passion for doing good'. Something is here left out. Over prose work representing both of these aspects (but not over his verse) Arnold's wit plays at times, aerating its seriousness and preventing its moderation from becoming insipid. If wit is not quite at the centre of his achievement, it is an attractive accompaniment of some very characteristic writing. Max Müller speaks of Arnold's 'Olympian manners' at Oxford. It would take a dull dog not to find endearing the Olympian impudence with which he begins an apology to Mr. Wright, a translator of the *Iliad*: 'One cannot always be studying one's own works, and I was really under the impression, till I saw Mr. Wright's complaint, that I had spoken of him with all respect . . .'

Ideally, detachment and zeal are the two sides of a single responsibility: the critic (using the term in the convenient Arnoldian sense to cover social commentator as well as literary critic) is loyal to the whole truth, but his judgement of what the public needs at a particular moment causes him to floodlight one fragment of it rather than another. Practically, however, there are sometimes two distinct responsibilities, and an awkward strain may be set up in the critic who is trying to do justice to both of them. Some confusions and peculiarities of emphasis in Arnold's prose—occasionally in the literary criticism, but more often elsewhere—show this clearly enough. There is some truth in the generalization that in the best of Arnold's poetry and literary criticism 'insight' is preferred to 'missionary zeal', and that an inverse order holds for the social and religious essays, but at best this is a rule with many exceptions. It may give us a reason for echoing the common opinion that Arnold's literary criticism and some of his poems[1] 'ought to be read first', or, to put it another way, that he is first and most importantly a

[1] Some only, for in many pieces—notably the sonnets of *New Poems* (1867)—the 'willed' or missionary element is uncomfortably strong.

poet-critic. But we should not in consequence think of the missionary aspect of Arnold's personality simply as a source of weakness: it was a source of both weakness and strength. It saved him from the typical solipsistic pedantries of the Ivory Tower critic; it seems to have supplied the motive-force for his devotion to his literary vocation (we think of Arnold rising earlier than the servants to read and write before the busy working-day of a school-inspector, and recall that temperamentally by his own confession a life of fly-fishing and reading the newspapers would have made him happy); and it may be connected with the common-sense that ballasts his other qualities, preventing his intelligence from feeding too much on abstractions, and his finesse from becoming too ethereally fine.

'From time to time, every hundred years or so, it is desirable that some critic shall appear to review the past of our literature, and set the poets and the poems in a new order . . . Dryden, Johnson and Arnold have each performed the task as well as human frailty will allow', Mr. T. S. Eliot has said, and today we may complete this short list with his own name. There are other poet-critics—Ben Jonson, Shelley, Coleridge (for many purposes the greatest of all English critics)—but within the exact scope of Mr. Eliot's intended meaning only three of the highest rank before the twentieth century. They are easily recognized. Each one in his own time singles himself out from his fellow-poets by a highly developed 'civic' sense on all matters touching the health of literature. Each, too, shows something of the flair of a public relations officer, so that he is readily accepted as the reigning King of the Sacred Wood, who personifies the unquestioned (because apparently self-evident) literary assumptions of the age. The relationship of a poet-critic to his immediate predecessor may be admiring, but it must be murderous (see Sir James Frazer's *The Golden Bough*): it has been noted that Mr. Eliot, while striving to be just, always has an edge in his voice when he speaks of Matthew Arnold (F. O. Matthiessen calls it 'deft, if inconspicuous sniping, kept up over quite a few years'). In this context the admission of the importance of Arnold's historical role is as handsome as it is convincing.

Matthew Arnold's appearance in the Victorian age at one remove from the present makes his importance much more than historical. He is nearer to us in time than other critics, and this in itself suggests that his criticism may still carry a 'live' charge, but the nearness is not simply a matter of chronology: it depends on a similarity between the Victorian age and our own, which underlies all the superficial differences, and it implies the existence of a real watershed between ancient and modern somewhere in the neighbourhood of Coleridge's *Biographia Literaria* (1817)—to put it as far back as possible. All great critics have their *aperçus* (to adopt Arnold's expression), which are timeless, but it is also the critic's function to organize these perceptions, to see how they best hang together in a pattern (the *ordo concatenatioque veri* is Arnold's name for it), and in the end much of every pattern is outmoded. An effort at translation from a dead tongue is needed when we consider the treatment of some of the classical questions of criticism in a seventeenth- or eighteenth-century critic, whereas Arnold's treatment is still in the vernacular in spite of the period flavour of a few of his usages. Equally important to our appreciation of him as a 'living' critic is a self-conscious approach which engages our natural sympathies. He performs and is the first spectator of his own performance, and this watchfulness smoothly dilates the reader's understanding of the meaning of critical activity.

> . . . judging is often spoken of as the critic's one business; and so in some sense it is; but the judgement which almost insensibly forms itself in a fair and clear mind, along with fresh knowledge, is the valuable one; and thus knowledge, and ever fresh knowledge, must be the critic's great concern for himself; and it is by communicating fresh knowledge, and letting his own judgement pass along with it, —but insensibly, and in the second place not the first, as a sort of companion and clue, not as an abstract lawgiver,—that he will generally do most good to his readers. Sometimes, no doubt, for the sake of establishing an author's place in literature, and his relation to

a central standard (and if this is not done, how are we to get at our *best in the world?*), criticism may have to deal with a subject-matter so familiar that fresh knowledge is out of the question, and then it must be all judgement; an enunciation and detailed application of principles. Here the great safeguard is never to let oneself become abstract, always to retain an intimate and lively consciousness of the truth of what one is saying, and, the moment this fails us, to be sure that something is wrong.

This is so true that in becoming obvious it has almost ceased to seem valuable, but it would not have crossed Dr. Johnson's mind to study himself so curiously or to explain himself in quite this way. It is a post-Coleridgean note.

Again, rightly considered, Arnold's tendency to stray from literary criticism into social and religious comment links him with Mr. Eliot and others among our contemporaries and distinguishes him from earlier critics—indeed, the tendency to stray seems to be a peculiar professional hazard in and after the Romantic period. To seek the reason would take us far, but I suppose it to be connected with the withering of customary certainties in literary criticism (for example, the obsolescence of 'kinds'), and this withering is part of a wider scepticism. When most questions are open questions, a critic may be hard put to it to deal with the propriety of a lyric's diction without raising the ghosts of moral and social issues. In Arnold and Eliot, and in a few capable modern critics on a smaller scale than either, the tendency to range widely marks the seriousness of the attention brought to bear on literature. They shoulder the same sort of white man's burden because they belong to the same cultural phase of the European mind.

Even an incomplete description of the variety of Arnold's attachments to the present must include one further illustration. For a generation or more now critics have discussed the 'dilemma' of the serious writer in a democracy which is for the most part complacently unaware that the education of taste lags hopelessly behind literacy. The problem, though smaller then, existed for some Victorians. 'You see before you, gentlemen,' Arnold told the Income Tax Commissioners at Edgware in 1870, 'what you have often heard of, *an unpopular author.*' It was more than a joke. He did not avoid public acclaim—on the contrary he wrote delightedly to his mother when he saw men with sandwich-boards in Regent Street advertising his essay on Marcus Aurelius—but he soberly realized how little excellence could mean to a mass-audience. 'Excellence dwells among rocks hardly accessible,' he declared, 'and a man must almost wear his heart out before he can reach her' (the easy, popular view had been taken by a lady from Ohio). He knew that his fastidiousness would appear to many both arrogant and lymphatic, but this did not deflect him from his course.[1] He also knew (sometimes with a jealous tincture) that his poetry would have to make its way slowly—general applause is perfunctory for verse that illustrates in Henry James's words 'a slight abuse of meagreness for distinction's sake'. Arnold's is an unobtrusive example of a literary integrity which a degree of isolation neither weakens nor sours: '. . . no one knows better than I do how little of a popular author I am,' he writes equably to a sister in 1874, 'but the thing is, I gradually produce a real effect, and the public acquires a kind of obscure interest in me as this gets to be perceived'. It would have meant something to Arnold that Walter Bagehot liked his poems (and took them with him on his honeymoon), or that Gerard Manley Hopkins sprang to his defence against the more conventional Robert Bridges ('I do not like to hear you calling Matthew Arnold Mr. Kidglove Cocksure . . . I am sure he is a rare genius and a great critic'), but it never disturbed him not to be the People's Candidate. The knowledge that the Victorian public was tepid about Arnold's gifts may have helped to keep his head above

---

[1] 'It is true that the critic has many temptations to go with the stream, to make one of the party of movement, one of these *terrae filii*; it seems ungracious to refuse to be a *terrae filius*, when so many excellent people are; but the critic's duty is to refuse, or, if resistance is vain, at least to cry with Obermann: "*Périssons en résistant.*"' 'The Function of Criticism at the Present Time', *Essays in Criticism*, First Series.

water when the high tide of disapproval of Victorianism rolled in during and after the first world war: more upholstered reputations sank waterlogged.

Matthew Arnold is certainly not a neglected 'great Victorian' in the present decade, but in one respect his reputation as a literary critic is less settled than it was a generation ago. This is a promising fact, for it is another indication that his influence is live, and at this interval from Mr. Eliot's accession to the kingship of the Sacred Wood it is becoming easier to see and acknowledge it. Arnold's historical position is disputed by nobody: he is a distinguished poet and a major critic, some of whose poems and literary essays are already secure English classics. What is disputed is the extent to which he can influence usefully the practice of criticism in our time. Now that Mr. Eliot's earlier critical work is in turn becoming historical, and we are less dazzled by the immediacy of his achievement as a poet and critic, Arnold's usefulness may be given broader limits and his authority may be expected to grow. This is fortunate. No two English critics complement each other so well in the whole of their critical performance; no other English critic has succeeded half so well as either in discovering the 'tone and temper' most exactly suited to the handling of literary subjects.

II

Arnold's writings have an inner logic shaped by personality and events. There need be nothing puzzling in the variety of subject-matter, style and intention found in such works as *Empedocles on Etna*, *A French Eton* and *Friendship's Garland* if we keep in mind the main stages of his career; and the tug-of-war of purposes in a particular essay makes sense more rapidly when it is recognized that duality haunts Arnold's thinking (Hellenism and Hebraism, Celt and Teuton, 'natural magic' and 'high seriousness', etc.) and is expressive of something in his nature. Arnold's own diagnosis of this 'something' cannot be disregarded:

> Ah! two desires toss about
> The poet's feverish blood.
> One drives him to the world without,
> And one to solitude

he tells us (in a stanza that illuminates the distinction between detachment and missionary zeal made in the previous section), and he is also the inventor of that striking phrase 'the dialogue of the mind with itself'. Certainly he did not think of his own nature as monolithic: 'I am fragments', he admitted to a favourite sister in 1853. Since the change from poetry to prose and the tendency to branch out from literary criticism into social and theological comment are both intimately connected with the development of Arnold's personality, something more must be said on this subject (even at the risk of over-simplification) when we have outlined his career.

Matthew Arnold was born on Christmas Eve, 1822, at Laleham-on-Thames, and died at the Dingle, Liverpool, on the fifteenth of April, 1888. He went to school at Winchester and Rugby and ended his Oxford years by election to an Oriel Fellowship (1845). In 1851 he wanted to marry and obtained through Lord Lansdowne, whose secretary he had been, the position of school inspector, which he held continuously until he retired in 1886. Various attempts to find a more congenial post all ended in frustration, and when his friend John Duke Coleridge was appointed Lord Chief Justice of Common Pleas in 1873, Arnold joked about the servants' hall being the right place for him if he paid a visit. He was a Balliol man, he declared sardonically, who had not 'got on'. A Civil List pension at sixty was the only official recognition of his talents. Unlike Tennyson or Browning, he had to make time for his literary work after dreary rounds of school visits and interminable report-writing.

> Here is my programme for this afternoon: Avalanches, the Steam Engine, the Thames, Indian Rubber, Bricks, the Battle of Poictiers,

Subtraction, the Reindeer, the Gunpowder Plot, the Jordan. Alluring is it not? Twenty minutes each, and the days of one's life are only three score years and ten.

He was a sympathetic rather than a stringent inspector, and some of his colleagues thought of him as an amateur after a lifetime of service. To put it euphemistically, there were jobs that would have suited him better. But against the suggestion of waste must be set whatever is valuable in the argument of *Culture and Anarchy* or *Friendship's Garland*: without Arnold's enforced intimacy with Dissent in the persons of Nonconformist school-managers and teachers, his portrait of the middle class would not have been a speaking likeness. His experiences as a school inspector helped to turn him into a critic of society.

The relief in the irksomely monotonous landscape of Arnold's official career comes from his tenure of the Oxford Chair of Poetry (1857-67),[1] which he held along with his bread-and-butter appointment, three educational missions to the continent (which sometimes allowed him to feel pleasantly ambassadorial), and a six-months lecture-tour to America in 1883-4. His regular 'anti-attrition' was in a most affectionate family-life, a diversity of friendships, solitary fishing, holidays abroad, favourite cats and dogs (including the superb Atossa—

> So Tiberius might have sat,
> Had Tiberius been a cat),

the Athenaeum, a little botanizing, tireless letter-writing, country-house visits, and wide reading in six languages. Most of the poetry was written before, almost all the prose after, 1857. The late eighteen-sixties and the eighteen-seventies were the years in which Arnold was most concerned in his writings with society and religion. Obvious trigger-causes were the troubles at the time of the second Reform Act (1867) and the 'crisis of belief' in the early eighteen-seventies.

[1] Arnold was the first professor to lecture in English instead of Latin. He drew enthusiastic audiences.

The man behind this brief dossier was tall and solidly-built, and affected a certain dandyism of manner which does not quite sort with the strength of his face—he inherited a 'Cornish' nose from his mother's side of the family—or its tinge of melancholy. As a young man he was thought handsome, and he long kept a youthful appearance and energy—it is not very fanciful to see a connection between his luxuriant black hair, hardly touched with grey in his late forties, and what Dallas calls 'the intense juvenility—a boy-power to the *nth*.' of his more ebullient prose. But this confident and youthfully energetic man had had an inauspicious childhood, which included the early wearing of iron leg-braces, a succession of illnesses, a bad stutter, and a loved and admired father's undisguised suspicion that he was lazy and irresponsible. Arnold's later wish to be 'papa's continuator' is rooted in the fact of Dr. Arnold's death before his son had done anything to 'justify' himself.

Probably Arnold's gaiety and fecklessness are best looked on as protective clothing for a genuine but never too sturdy poetic gift which he feared to expose to the onslaught of his father's earnestness. If so, it was also a highly effective piece of camouflage, for few of Arnold's intimates seem to have expected the seriousness of his first book of poems in 1849. Of course they may have been short-sighted: in 1846 George Sand was not deceived and described Arnold's appearance at Nohant as that of 'un Milton jeune et voyageant'. It is proper to assume that there was always an earnestness in the poet's nature which responded sympathetically to Dr. Arnold's fervour, but that he hid both it and his poetic seriousness behind a mask of frivolity in order to feel free enough and private enough to be a poet. This makes Dr. Arnold a more significant figure in the story of his son's development than anyone else—than even Arthur Clough, or 'K', or the shadowy Marguerite.

It is interesting to notice the places that were loved by Matthew Arnold. In England he was fondest of the Thames valley, the city of Oxford with the surrounding 'Scholar-

Gipsy' countryside, Loughrigg and the fells overlooking 'Fox How', the family home by the shallow Rotha on the outskirts of Ambleside (the clear running water which was Arnold's passion belongs to all three places and escapes into much of his characteristic poetic imagery). Abroad he was always happy in France and a small part of Switzerland glowed in his mind. Oxford and Thun[1] are more than place-names: they are mnemonics for recalling states of happiness associated with his fullest experience of feeling before 'settling down'.

> And yet what days were those, Parmenides!
> When we were young, when we could number friends
> In all the Italian cities like ourselves . . .

Few poets have ever been so miserably aware of the passage of time ('How life rushes away, and youth. One has dawdled and scrupled and fiddle-faddled—and it is all over') and the reiterated scoring in his notebooks of the phrase '*les saines habitudes de la maturité*' shows with what an effort at self-mastery he tried to welcome the bleakness of responsibility. Here again we seem to be close to Arnold's 'secret'. The divergent impulses that determine the dichotomies of his literary and social analysis exist because he is in two minds between whole-heartedly accepting maturity (and Dr. Arnold's mission) and the partial rejection implied by an agonized regret for youth and poetry and irresponsibility (which is the other face of detachment). At Thun in 1849 Arnold had two books with him, Béranger and Epictetus, and we find him writing to Clough that Béranger appealed to him less than formerly. It comes almost too pat to symbolize the victory of Stoic self-mastery over pleasure and poetry, a victory that governs Arnold's later development in the years of prose. But if poetry died, the poet in Arnold did not. He lived on to ensure the delicacy of the literary critic's insights, the social critic's unfailing contempt for optimistic claptrap. If Arnold

---

[1] Thun is the scene of the love affair with the French girl, Marguerite. It is simplest to say that we know nothing about it.

is a good critic, it is because regret kept open a line of communication with his poetic past, because 'character' was never quite free from the promptings of 'temperament'. When he tells us that the work of the nineteenth century in literature is work for the 'imaginative reason', he is asserting that a control which is never imperilled is likely to become obtuse. Even a fifth column may be useful in keeping a government on its toes.

'They went forth to battle and they always fell', Matthew Arnold quotes in speaking of the Celts, and in the opposition established by him between Celt and Teuton we have another avatar of the conflict between poetic temperament and 'moral' character. 'Natural magic' is Celtic and a happiness of poetic style, whereas Teutons have no sense of style in spite of being worthy, forthright, and necessary. 'I have a great *penchant* for the Celtic races, with their melancholy and unprogressiveness,' Arnold wrote to Lady de Rothschild, and it is curious how emphatically in this instance he repudiated any suggestion that Dr. Arnold might have shared his sentiments (see *Letters of Matthew Arnold*, II, p. 320). The Celt strained against 'the despotism of fact' as the poet in Arnold's make-up struggled against accepting maturity. When Arnold insisted that his father had not really understood the Celts, he was insisting that his father had not understood him. He was also saying obliquely what he once said openly: 'My dear father had many virtues, but he was not a poet'. Several critics have noticed that Sohrab's death in the poem at the hands of his father, Rustum, is a type of Arnold's sacrifice of the poetic temperament so that he may identify himself more closely with his father's moral earnestness. What is also to be remarked if we are to do full justice to the situation is Sohrab's profound admiration and affection for Rustum and the poignancy of his regret for the final loss of

Youth and bloom and this delightful world.

Matthew Arnold, as W. H. Auden says, 'thrust his gift in prison till it died', but he did it out of love. Perhaps this explains why his maturity is so little cross-grained, and why he is almost incapable of a false note when he sings of renunciation and unwished necessity.

In his finest short story, 'The Point of It', Mr. E. M. Forster pessimistically argues that 'everyone grows hard or soft as he grows old', and Arnold himself did not have many illusions about the irony of the 'gifts reserved for age'. There are, I think, a few signs of hardening in the later Arnold (far fewer than in most of his contemporaries): a crotchetiness about the Irish question in the eighteen-eighties, which found fuel in his old antipathy to Gladstone; traces of personal agitation when he accuses the French of worshipping the goddess Lubricity; an ill-natured stiffness in one or two remarks about Keats and Shelley (with the connotation of an almost reflex disapproval of sexuality); some absurdity in his ducking respect for German 'higher critics of the Bible'.[1] But these signs do not add up to much, and it is pleasanter to stress how open to fresh impressions, how '*ondoyant et divers*' as a critic, he remained to the end. He conquered regret without turning his heart into a stone, and the last pages of his *Letters* show us a man who deserves admiration—shrewd, capable, deeply affectionate, still interested in everything about him, and honourably civilized.

III

Matthew Arnold had written some verses before he went to school at Winchester, and a few pieces (including some 'animal' poems and the frigid 'Westminster Abbey') belong to the eighteen-eighties, but all the work by which he is still

---

[1] Contrast Arnold's blithe impatience with them as a younger man. In 1850 he writes to Clough about F. W. Newman's *Phases of Faith:*

One would think to read him that enquiries into articles, biblical inspiration, etc., etc., were as much the natural functions of a man as to eat and copulate. This sort of man is only possible in Great Britain and Germany, thanks be to God for it.

known was produced between 1845 and 1867. Indeed *New
Poems* of the latter year contained such a thin harvest for the
second decade that it had to be filled out with 'Empedocles
on Etna', reprinted for the first time since 1852 at the
request—as Arnold was careful to tell his readers—of a
'man-of-genius, Mr. Robert Browning'. But, if few poems
were composed between 1857 and 1867, certain of them were
among Arnold's most finished work, notably 'Thyrsis',
often considered to be his poetic masterpiece. It is part of
Arnold's 'tragedy' as a poet that he reached his fullest command of expressive power when his creative impulse was
already failing—a fact noticed with laconic bitterness in
'The Progress of Poesy'. Arnold's first two volumes were *The
Strayed Reveller* (1849) and *Empedocles on Etna* (1852). The
various collections issued between 1852 and *New Poems* lean
heavily on the two early books, both of which were with-
drawn by Arnold after very few copies had been sold. For
example, *Poems* (1853) contains lyrics from both volumes, as
well as the famous Preface defending the suppression of
'Empedocles on Etna', 'Sohrab and Rustum', written to
illustrate—in the words of the Preface—'that the action
itself, its selection and construction, . . . is . . . all-important',
'The Scholar Gipsy', and various other new pieces which are
less well-known. Arnold liked to play with his poems when
he was unable to write many new ones, suppressing and
reviving now one and now another, and tinkering with their
order in different collections, so that the make-up of his suc-
cessive books of verse is confusing; but these changes hardly
affect our estimate of him as a poet.

It is clear from *The Strayed Reveller* that a naked ethical
intention intrudes into Arnold's poems from the beginning
and often does them injury. 'Intrude' may seem to be an
odd word to employ in connection with an intention so
typical of Arnold and so usually present in his work, but I
use it advisedly to suggest that his truest note as a poet
depends on qualities of feeling at war with ethical impulse.
This is evident in Arnold's response to his own poems.

'Empedocles on Etna' is rejected for reasons that may be summarized by saying that Arnold thought his poetic drama would dispirit rather than fortify (though we may well think him wrong in this judgement of its probable effect). There is another weak aesthetic choice for 'heroic' moral reasons in a letter to Clough: 'I am glad you like the Gipsy Scholar—but what does it *do* for you . . . in its poor way I think Sohrab and Rustum *animates*—the Gipsy Scholar at best awakes a pleasing melancholy . . . But this is not what we want'. Arnold was quite wrong. What his readers have always wanted from him is more poems like 'The Scholar Gipsy' or the Cadmus and Harmonia episode from 'Empedocles on Etna', that is to say, more pieces in which he realizes his poetic vocation without interference. Caught faithless between two worlds and 'wavering between the profit and the loss', his vocation was to sing of melancholy and indecision, to express the sad confusion of desires which find no sufficient object, to create for us the self-conscious animal whose thinking runs ahead and undermines his present experience of happiness. The best poetry is a time-haunted, dimly lit *campagna* of regret, for all Arnold's wish that it should be something different. Not that the regret is simple and unmixed. The bracing of moral intention is never completely absent from the pieces I have in mind, but in them it appears inoffensively, and always as a minor constituent, to make the regret stoically tightlipped, to produce an effect which I can only describe as one of ravaged composure. The best poetry, then, is written by a 'Celt' and pierces by its understatement. When the 'Teuton' shoulders aside the 'Celt', and morality takes charge, we get the priggish artificiality of 'East London' or 'The Second Best':

> Not here, O Apollo!
> Are haunts meet for thee;

while in other poems, undoubtedly superior but still liable to worry us, it is impossible to say whether 'Teuton' or 'Celt' has gained the upper hand. 'Palladium' may be cited as an example. A final class consists of poems innocent of a conscious moral intention but into whose conception too strong a willed element has entered, and we have then the blameless nullities of *Merope* and 'Balder Dead'. 'Sohrab and Rustum' is another 'willed' poem, but, as I have already indicated, it managed to attach itself to Arnold's emotional life without his knowledge, and it draws whatever effectiveness it has from this source. In so brief an account of the poetry it is fair to say that Arnold's deepest poetic intuition is of

> The something that infects the world,

and that he never makes us anxious for him as an artist when he writes of it (for instance in 'The Sick King in Bokhara'), or nostalgically of loss, or—at his most positive—of fortitude and resignation: on the other hand, the attempts to whistle up a simple cheerfulness are invariably poetic failures—even the modified optimism at the end of 'Obermann Once More' has a counterfeit ring.

When Arnold discovered how dark were his gifts as a poet, he stopped writing poetry—an action for which we are prepared after the rejection of 'Empedocles on Etna'. In his *Letters* the pathos of his middle-aged regret for the loss of his Ariel, whom he had handed over to perpetual confinement in the charge of a moralist, is real and moving. But as a poet he had then done what it was in him to do. In 'Empedocles on Etna', 'Resignation' and 'The Sick King in Bokhara', in passages from 'Sohrab and Rustum' and the unequal 'Tristram and Iseult', in many of the shorter lyrics, and in almost all the elegiac pieces (including 'Thyrsis' and 'The Scholar Gipsy'), we have his most genuine note. 'Arnold is more intimate with us than Browning, more intimate than Tennyson ever is except at moments,' Mr. Eliot observes justly, and it must be of some of these pieces that he is thinking. Henry James certainly had them in mind when he spoke with his customary exactitude of Arnold's 'minor magic' and of his sensitive touching of 'the particular ache, or regret, or conjecture, to which poetry is supposed to

address itself'. In a number of these successes it must be
admitted that Arnold incurs the censure that he himself pro-
nounced on those who substitute 'thinking aloud' in poetry
for 'making something'—in his view a tendency encouraged
by Wordsworth. A too casual 'thinking aloud' seems to be
the fault of 'The Future', 'The Buried Life' and 'The Youth
of Man', which are ramshackle in structure, and we recognize the support that the pastoral convention gave Arnold in
'Thyrsis', and the advantages that he found in a well-defined
subject in 'A Southern Night' and 'Stanzas from the Grande
Chartreuse'. But these structural faults weaken without dis-
abling the poems in which they occur, and it may be claimed
for these pieces, as perhaps on behalf of the greater number
of Arnold's poems, that they are more satisfying at the tenth
than at the first reading, and more endearing than many
Victorian poems which wear their too obvious hearts on
gaudier sleeves. Let us set down here a typical penny-plain
passage of Arnold's verse:

> Rais'd are the dripping oars—
> Silent the boat: the lake,
> Lovely and soft as a dream,
> Swims in the sheen of the moon.
> The mountains stand at its head
> Clear in the pure June night,
> But the valleys are flooded with haze.
> Rydal and Fairfield are there;
> In the shadow Wordsworth lies dead.
> So it is, so it will be for aye.
> Nature is fresh as of old,
> Is lovely: a mortal is dead.

These verses chosen at random are in a quiet way impressive.
There is no Keats in them and little Wordsworth. The vocabulary is simple, the moonlight and water are among Arnold's
most pleasing stage-properties, even the hint of a mechanical
quality in the rhythm (which seems to be accepted as if to
slight any charge of extravagance) is, I think, effective, and
the whole verse-paragraph lucidly projects the constraint put

upon emotion. A reader may not be attracted by these un-assuming lines and still find it possible to admire 'Thyrsis' or 'Dover Beach', but I do not think he can be said to have understood Arnold's poetic character unless they engage his sympathies.

Clearly an informed appreciation of Arnold as a poet must recognize the severe limitations of his gift. He has little poetic *élan* (the possession of which he envied Byron), slight ease, rare incandescence, no prodigality in phrase or meta-phor: he spends his poetic income thriftily. He makes too much of excellence of subject, and one has unhappy memories of Haydon's historical paintings and the old recipes for an epic—this is not to deny the significance of his protest against the over-valuing of the poetic 'moment' and poetic frills by the 'Spasmodic' admirers of Keats in Arnold's own day. He is completely undramatic—the banality of the dialogue in the second part of 'Tristram and Iseult' is disconcerting—and lack of dramatic sense narrows his scope as a narrative poet. He is uninventive in verse-forms, limited in colour and vocabulary in all but a very few pieces, repetitive in theme and situation, too often seriously insensitive to the sound of his poems—such a line as the following in a poem that is something of a showpiece—

But when the moon their hollows lights

—is far from unusual, and Tennyson would have shuddered at it. Yet Arnold triumphs over his maladroitness and unob-trusively creates a presumption in his own favour by the time we are ready to sit down in judgement. He is like a handicapped man whom his disabilities have taught a dis-tinctive spryness and resource, and for whom we are pre-pared to make allowances. He triumphs by a feeling for poetic decorum in which many other Victorians were exas-peratingly deficient, by his intelligent command of 'tone and temper', by an intimidating kind of honesty—for he steadily refuses to varnish his unease. He is an unfinished Leopardi comfortless in the Victorian Canaan. We understand at once what Hopkins means when he says that sometimes Arnold's poems 'seem to have all the ingredients of poetry without quite being it', and we agree with him again when he continues, '. . . still they do not leave off of being, as the French say, very beautiful'. When the devil's advocate has done his worst, 'Empedocles on Etna' remains perhaps the best long poem by a Victorian, while in 'Thyrsis', 'The Scholar Gipsy' and three or four shorter pieces (which do not include the overpraised and rather vapid 'Requiescat') Arnold's poetry is no longer hobbled and he escapes from his limitations, as a stutterer may escape in dreams, into speech of unimpeded fluency. Arnold argued that his poetry represented 'the main line of modern development' in his day and that this would finally recommend it to attention. He was prepared to await his turn. There is certainly a level of approach at which we can link many of Arnold's poems with Clough's 'Dipsychus' and Melville's *Clarel* under the heading of Victorian 'poetry of doubt'—it may be useful to think of his influence on A. E. Housman and Edwin Arlington Robinson—but I have here preferred to suggest that his complaint against

> . . . this strange disease of modern life
> With its sick hurry, its divided aims . . .

betrays a more fundamental discontent. As a poet he is always, it seems to me, the romantic Celt struggling against the 'despotism of fact'. His muted nostalgia is for a wholeness and simplicity of experience that never was. By any normal system of moral book-keeping it may be reprehensible, and clearly the more robust comment on experience is '. . . if you don't like it, you can get on with it', but any man who has not buried his youth too deeply can understand Arnold. What evidence there is points to his being more widely read today than any other mid-Victorian poet.

IV

In 1853 Matthew Arnold wrote to Arthur Clough:

> I catch myself desiring now at times political life, and this and that; and I say to myself you do not desire these things because you are really adapted to them, and therefore the desire for them is merely contemptible—and it is so.

Ten years later we find him writing to his mother:

> It is very animating to think that one at last has a chance of getting at the English public. Such a public as it is and such a work as one wants to do with it.

It is the gap between the self-regarding ethic of the first statement and the eager wish to interfere of the second that explains the plausibility of the late Professor E. K. Brown's *Matthew Arnold: a study in conflict*, the most acute study yet of Arnold as a prose-writer, critic and controversialist, in which it is argued that the objectivity of Arnold's criticism is flawed by his wish to be a moral leader, and that in the social essays 'detachment' is often most flagrantly only a wraith-like appearance. In many places in Arnold's prose, Professor Brown held, it is proper to talk of a 'strategy of disinterestedness', for the apparent candour and urbanity are almost exclusively at the service of an 'interested disposition'.

Once or twice already I have expressed reservations about this view. Evidently the poet speaks in the first letter quoted above, the son of Dr. Arnold in the second. But to agree with many other commentators that there is a conflict in Arnold, and that it casts a shadow over his writings, need not lead us to assume with Professor Brown that a crusading impulse is incompatible with a local and particular objectivity: if this were really so, one would expect Arnold's criticism to have some of the polemical extravagance of Ruskin's or the later Carlyle's. This view also fails to recognize how much of Arnold's most 'detached' literary criticism we may owe to his missionary impulse: to put this naively, Arnold might very well have kept his *aperçus* to himself if he had not felt them to be useful when he began at the call of duty 'to pull out a few more stops in that powerful but at present somewhat narrow-toned organ, the modern Englishman'.

Arnold's prose works in the incomplete Macmillan collected edition run to ten volumes—this is to disregard his letters, and there are uncollected papers to fill two volumes more—and, within the confines of the present essay, I can hardly even signal the inclusiveness and authority of Arnold's interpretation of his age, or hope to submit Professor Brown's thesis to the examination that it deserves: instead I must say that in my opinion Arnold ordinarily succeeds in finding a third way between a limiting involvement in practical issues and a lack of interest in the social implications of his ideas. His 'detachment' is more than a confidence-man's patter. If a 'strategy of disinterestedness' exists in Arnold's wish to speak calmly and without rancour, the wish is in no sense Jesuitical: it stands both for the respect with which the writer approaches the truth and for the power of his writings to charm an audience. To a dispassionate reader 'The Function of Criticism at the Present Time' in *Essays in Criticism* (1865) is quite explicit on the double need for disinterestedness and moral engagement. It tells us what Arnold thought he was doing and, in nine cases out of ten, it is what he was doing.

At this point it is obvious that limited space must enforce a paralysing generality on any attempt to survey Arnold's prose. I propose to escape from this difficulty by indicating the motivation of Arnold's criticism as a whole, selecting a few topics, mostly in the literary criticism, for a rapid closer look. Such a bias may be justified because the literary criticism is in fact more often studied than the social and religious writings, and because it is superior to them in freshness, confidence and ease—this is more especially true of the earlier critical essays. To come to *On Translating Homer* (1861) or *On the Study of Celtic Literature*

(1867) straight from the world of the poetry, or to turn back to them after being immersed in *Literature and Dogma* (1873) or *Last Essays on Church and Religion* (1877), is to find one-self in an atmosphere with an exhilaratingly high proportion of oxygen. This mood of the early criticism (with the exception perhaps of the valuable but too obviously instructive 1853 Preface) exhibits publicly the excitement at discovering an unexpected second vocation which is characteristic of so many of Arnold's private letters to Clough—a correspon-dence second only to Keats's *Letters* in English literature for its sharp insights and its fascinating glimpse at the elliptical gambolling of a free intelligence. A famous passage in Sainte-Beuve's *Portraits Contemporains*, in which he speaks of a critical vocation often being concealed in youth by poetry and of criticism as '*un pis-aller honorable*', apparently came to Arnold—increasingly aware that his talent though 'distinguished' was 'stinted'—with the force of a revelation.

The most general motive of Arnold's criticism is ethical. He is almost without metaphysical passion, which may be the fundamental reason for F. H. Bradley's dislike of the religious writings, but his ethical passion is unmistakable. To Arnold metaphysical reasoning was simply methodical self-bewilderment, but he had as strongly as George Eliot the conviction that the moral law exists and speaks unequi-vocally in experience. On the one side, then, religion was ceremonial practices, which he supported *because* they were absurd—much as Bagehot defended the decorative elements in the English constitution as 'social cement'; on the other side, religion was morality, which religious feeling could 'light up' and transform into a driving-force. The rest was 'over-belief' (*Aberglaube*). In the eyes of orthodox churchmen Arnold was 'widening the rat-hole in the Temple', but he saw himself as a conservative. Miracles did not occur, theo-logy was a pseudo-science, and literary tact discerned that theologians had done enormous violence to the loose figura-tive language of the Bible—language never meant to be precise, but 'thrown out' at objects of consciousness 'not fully grasped'. If the philosopher F. H. Bradley could tartly describe the God of Arnold's writings as no more than 'an hypostasized copy-book heading', Arnold was quite sure that the traditional idea of God arose from a failure to distinguish the scientific and poetic uses of language. Arnold believed that he was defending religion by surrendering its untenable outposts, but we are more likely to feel that he was attempting—in an adaptation of Hartley Coleridge's phrase about Wordsworth—to smuggle Spinoza into the pulpit in a curate's ragged surplice.

What made Arnold so keen to 'save' religion from its friends was his conviction of its social importance. Numerous impulses (including the religious one), he argued, must be met for man's 'harmonious development':

> Money-making is not enough by itself. Industry is not enough by itself. Seriousness is not enough by itself . . . The need in man for intellect and knowledge, his desire for beauty, his instinct for society, and for pleasurable and graceful forms of society, require to have their stimulus felt also, felt and satisfied.

This is the master-thought of Arnold's social writings. His experiences as a school inspector had made him peculiarly aware that social and political influence was passing into the hands of the middle class, which was quite unready for power and even unsuited to it. He could not turn hopefully from the Philistines to the old aristocracy. With a cool eye for a real lord and no faith in the Carlylean alternative of an industrial 'nobility', he confided in an ideal of democratic state action—and the state's first responsibility was to be in the field of education. The matter was urgent. The upper classes were materialized, the middle class was vulgarized, the lower classes were brutalized (the famous division into Barbarians, Philistines and Populace). The state was the only possible source of national unity, but for a combination of reasons it was regarded with deep suspicion, and this made Arnold over-emphatic and something less than 'disinterested' in certain pages of *Culture and Anarchy* (1869).[1] The battle-cry of Hebraism and Hellenism was important for all Englishmen, most important for the Philistines. Hebraism characterized the narrow life of that typical Philistine, the thrifty, earnest Dissenter who divided his time between counting-house and chapel, sure of his solvency in this world and salvation in the next. He stood sadly in need of hellenization—culture might woo him from his dreary tea-meetings and Temperance lectures (with lantern-slides), his hymnal and his balance-sheets. Culture might induce him to re-examine his stock notions and habits, might broaden his religious sympathies, might ultimately shame him into dissatisfaction with a 'dismal, illiberal life' in Sheffield or Camberwell. In Arnold's opinion culture spoke most persuasively through literature.[2]

This explanation of the main motive of Arnold's social thinking does not bring in all his important social ideas—it omits, for example, his stress on equality, which is the subject of an essay in 1878—but it is enough to show the link between the social and the literary criticism. In 'The Function of Criticism at the Present Time' the failure of the Romantic poets in spite of their prodigious creative talent is ascribed to a weakness in the surrounding cultural atmosphere. For a great creative epoch 'two powers must concur, the power of the man and the power of the moment'. Arnold sees a critical effort in his own generation as the necessary

---

[1] The appeal to find in the state a collective representation of the 'best self' in every man has been supposed by some writers to have dangerous Hegelian overtones, but it was really no more than a political application of the religious idea of 'dying to the old Adam'—the state was to charge itself with supporting the 'disinterested' ethical self of which every man was capable. It is quite wrong to suppose that Arnold had a sneaking weakness for authoritarianism—he came to look on Carlyle as a 'moral desperado', and he was one of the few literary men who had no patience with the rowdy defence of Governor Eyre. Arnold had much the same view of the state as Dr. Arnold, and both looked back to Burke.

[2] *Culture and Anarchy* (1869), *Mixed Essays* (1879), and the satirical extravaganza *Friendship's Garland* (1871), are the most valuable of the social writings.

spade-work for a new creative age. It is the critic's job by making available 'the best that is known and thought in the world' to produce a 'current of fresh and true ideas' in society. If he fails, the poet is unable to realize all his gifts or to produce work of the first order. The critic, then, is much more than a judge. At one and the same time he is a kind of midwife to artistic genius and the mediator between the artist and the general public.

Nothing takes precedence of the critic's function to supply 'fresh knowledge', and in speaking of this Arnold is a European.

> But, after all, the criticism I am really concerned with . . . is a criticism which regards Europe as being, for intellectual and spiritual purposes, one great confederation, bound to a joint action and working to a common result; and whose members have, for their proper outfit, a knowledge of Greek, Roman, and Eastern antiquity, and of one another.

Occasionally scholars have regretted the essays on minor figures of foreign literature (Joubert, Amiel, etc.), as if they were a frivolous turning aside from the truly important, but Arnold has a ready answer. He is bringing to light comparatively unknown excellence, and, while he is so engaged, he avoids a very real danger: he runs no risk of interesting readers in his treatment of the subject at the expense of the subject itself (how much modern criticism of Shakespeare or Milton is X's judgement of Y's opinion of Z's remarks). Arnold thought the critic should explore widely and 'welcome everything that is good', but this did not blur for him the distinction between 'excellent and inferior, sound and unsound and only half-sound'. This distinction was of 'paramount importance'. Arnold's severity can be measured by his remarks on the limiting effects of Milton's temper on his genius, or his disquiet when faced with the uneven copiousness of Shakespeare's style.

Two of the three most significant aspects which identify ⦿ Arnold's critical practice have now been mentioned— namely, the concern with fresh information, and the need to discriminate between what is excellent and what is less good while welcoming positive excellence even in unusual or subordinate 'kinds'. The third aspect has to do with his wholesome sense of the difficulty of criticism. His preference for the judgement that forms itself insensibly in the critic's mind (with its corollary that for the reader the critic's opinion should appear simply to make explicit what is implicit in the accompanying information) is clearly connected with his awareness of the delicacy of the critical act.

> To handle these matters properly there is needed a poise so perfect that the least overweight in any direction tends to destroy the balance... To press to the sense of the thing itself with which one is dealing, not to go off on some collateral issue about the thing, is the hardest matter in the world. The 'thing itself' with which one is here dealing, the critical perception of poetic truth, is of all things the most volatile, elusive, and evanescent; by even pressing too impetuously after it, one runs the risk of losing it. The critic of poetry should have the finest tact, the nicest moderation, the most free, flexible, and elastic spirit imaginable; he should be indeed the 'ondoyant et divers', the *undulating and diverse* being of Montaigne.

Again, the care to reach the truth exemplified in this passage is certainly not unrelated to Arnold's desire to 'charm'. To charm meant to investigate his subject in such a way that the reader's own prejudices should not be interposed between him and what the critic had taken so much trouble to say.

Around this just and comprehensive understanding of the critic's task the counters of Arnold's criticism—'high seriousness', 'natural magic', 'the grand style', '*Architectonicè*', etc. —group themselves, not as precise meanings, but as instruments he found useful in obtaining a view of the truth, and in creating for his readers an intimate sense of his critical adequacy. Arnold's prose style should be noticed in a study of his technique of persuasion. It has several modes including the lyrical and the wilfully impertinent—both are illustrated in the preface to the second edition (1869) of *Essays in Criticism*—but the usual middle style resembles Newman's prose in its subtle vitality. Perhaps the similarity is more than stylistic, and it may be right to be reminded of Newman's psychological account of what we do when we 'reason' or 'believe' in reading Arnold's description of what constitutes the critical act.

In what has been said there is a basis of justification for calling Arnold a great critic. The argument would need to be completed in a fuller discussion by an analysis of his remarks on Homer, Dante, Shakespeare, Milton, Voltaire, Gray and Dr. Johnson, Leopardi, Heine and the English Romantic poets—to mention only a few of those to whom he paid attention. In some instances the necessary assembling of scattered references has yet to be attempted; and perhaps some modern critics have been over-hasty in giving us Arnold's opinion on a particular topic without making a real effort to discover what it was. It is possible that on many of these subjects we might not express ourselves exactly as he did, but this is unimportant. Occasionally—for example, in discussing Byron as a man of feeling—he misses the point, but quite often he comes very close to a reputable contemporary opinion: I would cite in evidence his parenthetic observation that Shelley's 'natural magic' is almost entirely in his rhythm and hardly at all in his language; or, again, the several judgements on Goethe, which add up to a very respectable whole view (and what a triumph of 'detachment' in its Victorian context his reserved attitude to *Wilhelm Meister* represents). Such successes more than cancel his too much paraded critical howlers, some of which are susceptible of a kind of defence. For example, Arnold's opinion that Dryden and Pope are 'classics of our prose' shows that he failed to appreciate the Augustan achievement in poetry, but it pithily expresses that turning down of the imaginative lamps which any reader must feel as he moves from a study of the great Renaissance poets to the poetic literature of the late seventeenth and early eighteenth centuries.

In estimating Arnold's special importance as a critic today, debate about the supersession of this or that opinion is unhelpful. What matters is his example of serious critical responsibility. Literary criticism was not a matter of self-expression for Arnold. He directs attention at his subject and away from his own dexterity. He commits himself unambiguously and in an 'unprofessional' language, and he makes no secret of the relationship between his literary opinions and his views on the 'great questions' of life and society. His candour is never ill-humoured. In all these respects Mr. T. S. Eliot is his only living rival. I have already said that these two major critics complement each other in a variety of ways. No better exercise for sharpening the wits can be imagined than the setting up of one against the other on any topic on which they overlap. For a generation now we have used Mr. Eliot to correct Matthew Arnold. It is useful to remember that the process can run in reverse.

MATTHEW ARNOLD
A Select Bibliography

(Place of publication London, unless stated otherwise)

Readers should supplement this selective book-list by consulting *The Cambridge Bibliography of English Literature* (1940), Vol. III, and the bibliographies given in several of the books listed under 'Some Biographical and Critical Works'.

Bibliographies:

THE BIBLIOGRAPHY OF MATTHEW ARNOLD, by T. B. Smart (1892). Revised and expanded in Vol. XV of the *Works*, 1904.

CATALOGUE OF THE ASHLEY LIBRARY, by T. J. Wise, Vol. I (1922).

BIBLIOGRAPHIES OF TWELVE VICTORIAN AUTHORS, by T. G. Ehrsam, R. H. Deily and R. M. Smith, New York (1936).

See also 'Notes Towards a Matthew Arnold Bibliography' by M. Mainwaring, *Modern Philology*, Vol. 49 (1952).

Collected Editions:

1. *Poetry and Prose*

THE WORKS OF MATTHEW ARNOLD, 15 vols. (1903–4).
Contains the poems (I and II), the prose works (III–XII), and the letters edited by G. W. E. Russell (XIII–XV), but omits various uncollected essays.

2. *Poetry*

POEMS: A NEW AND COMPLETE EDITION, Boston (1856).

POEMS, 2 vols. (1869).
Vol. I. Narrative and elegiac. Vol. II. Dramatic and lyric.

POEMS. NEW AND COMPLETE EDITION, 2 vols. (1877).
Vol. I. Early poems, narrative poems and sonnets. Vol. II. Lyric, dramatic and elegiac poems.

POEMS, 3 vols. (1885).
Vol. I. Early poems, narrative poems and sonnets. Vol. II. Lyric and elegiac poems. Vol. III. Dramatic and later poems. The first comprehensive edition, and the last edition to be supervised by Arnold.

THE POETICAL WORKS (1890).
> The Globe Edition.

THE POEMS, 1840–1867, Oxford (1909).
> Edited by H. S. M[itford]. Introduction by A. T. Quiller-Couch.
> Reprinted seven times until 1940. Reissued as *The Poetical Works*
> (with the poems written after 1867) in 1942. Reprinted 1945.

THE POETICAL WORKS (1950).
> Edited by C. B. Tinker and H. F. Lowry, with critical apparatus
> supplying 'a full record of the successive alterations of the text
> from the manuscripts (when such are known) onwards through
> the various editions'. This is now the standard edition.

3. *Prose*

WORKS, 10 vols. (1883–1903).
> The Smith, Elder & Co. 'Popular' edition contains all the impor-
> tant prose volumes except *Essays in Criticism*, First and Second
> Series, and *Discourses in America*.

ESSAYS BY MATTHEW ARNOLD, Oxford (1914).
> Contains *Essays in Criticism*, First Series, *On Translating Homer*
> (with F. W. Newman's reply), *On Translating Homer: Last
> Words*, and five essays 'hitherto uncollected' in Great Britain.
> Four of these essays had already appeared in the American *Essays
> in Criticism*, Third Series (see below).

Selections:

SELECTED POEMS (1878).
> Selected by Arnold himself.

PASSAGES FROM THE PROSE WRITINGS (1880).
> Selected by Arnold himself.

MATTHEW ARNOLD: POETRY AND PROSE (1954).
> The Reynard Library edition by J. Bryson. A comprehensive selec-
> tion which includes some of Arnold's letters.

Verse and prose selections are numerous. Selections from the verse
have appeared in the Temple Classics, the World's Classics, The
Muses' Library, Everyman's Library, The Crown Classics, The Poets
on the Poets Series (1948) etc. The most recent selection is in Penguin
Poets (1954). Among prose selections the following should be noted:
Selections from the Prose Writings, edited by L. E. Gates, New York

(1898); *Selections from Matthew Arnold's Prose*, edited by D. C. Somervell (1924); and *Representative Essays of Matthew Arnold*, edited by E. K. Brown, Toronto (1936), which contains some 'reprinted passages' from early editions.

Separate Works:

ALARIC AT ROME: a prize poem, recited in Rugby School, Rugby (1840). *Verse.*

A facsimile was privately printed by T. J. Wise, 1893.

CROMWELL: a prize poem, recited in the Theatre, Oxford. Oxford (1843). *Verse.*

THE STRAYED REVELLER, AND OTHER POEMS, by 'A' (1849). *Verse.*

EMPEDOCLES ON ETNA, AND OTHER POEMS, by 'A' (1852). *Verse.*

POEMS, A New Edition (1853). *Verse.*

Reprints poems from 1849 and 1852. Includes a critical preface and, among the new poems, 'Sohrab and Rustum' and 'The Scholar Gipsy'.

POEMS, Second Edition (1854). *Verse.*

Without five poems included in the first edition, but with the addition of 'A Farewell', first published in 1852, and a further brief preface.

POEMS, Second Series (1855). *Verse.*

Reprints poems from 1849 and 1852. Includes 'Balder Dead' and one other new poem.

POEMS, Third Edition (1857). *Verse.*

A reprint of the 1854 collection, with a new piece in the 'Switzerland' group.

MEROPE: a tragedy (1858). *Verse.*

With a preface. There is an annotated edition by J. C. Collins, Oxford (1906).

ENGLAND AND THE ITALIAN QUESTION (1859). *Politics.*

Edited by M. Bevington, Durham, N.C. (1953), with 'Matthew Arnold and the Italian Question' by J. Fitzjames Stephen.

THE POPULAR EDUCATION OF FRANCE, WITH NOTICES OF THAT OF HOLLAND AND SWITZERLAND (1861). *Education.*

ON TRANSLATING HOMER: Three Lectures given at Oxford (1861). *Literary criticism.*

Edited by W. H. D. Rouse, 1905.

ON TRANSLATING HOMER: LAST WORDS: a lecture given at Oxford (1862). *Literary criticism.*

A FRENCH ETON; OR, MIDDLE CLASS EDUCATION AND THE STATE (1864). *Education.*

ESSAYS IN CRITICISM (1865). *Literary criticism.*
Known as 'First Series'. The second edition has a condensed preface, the third edition contains an additional essay 'A Persian Passion Play'. There is a useful annotated edition by C. A. Miles and L. Smith, Oxford (1918).

ON THE STUDY OF CELTIC LITERATURE (1867). *Literary criticism.*
Edited by A. Nutt, 1910.

NEW POEMS (1867). *Verse.*
Includes 'Empedocles on Etna', reprinted for the first time since 1852, and six other pieces which had already appeared in a collection.

SCHOOLS AND UNIVERSITIES ON THE CONTINENT (1868). *Education.*

CULTURE AND ANARCHY: AN ESSAY IN POLITICAL AND SOCIAL CRITICISM (1869). *Social criticism.*
An excellent edition by J. Dover Wilson, Cambridge (1931).

ST. PAUL AND PROTESTANTISM; WITH AN INTRODUCTION ON PURITANISM AND THE CHURCH OF ENGLAND (1870). *Religion.*
The Popular Edition of 1887 contains a new preface and 'A Comment on Christmas'.

FRIENDSHIP'S GARLAND: BEING THE CONVERSATIONS, LETTERS, AND OPINIONS OF THE LATE ARMINIUS, BARON VON THUNDER-TEN-TRONCKH. COLLECTED AND EDITED, WITH A DEDICATORY LETTER TO ADOLESCENS LEO, ESQ., OF 'THE DAILY TELEGRAPH' (1871). *Satirical extravaganza.*

LITERATURE AND DOGMA. AN ESSAY TOWARDS A BETTER APPREHENSION OF THE BIBLE (1873). *Religion.*
The Popular Edition of 1883 is condensed.

HIGHER SCHOOLS AND UNIVERSITIES IN GERMANY (1874). *Education.*
A reprint of the German chapters of *Schools and Universities on the Continent.*

GOD AND THE BIBLE. A REVIEW OF OBJECTIONS TO 'LITERATURE AND DOGMA' (1875). *Religion.*
The Popular Edition of 1884 is condensed.

LAST ESSAYS ON CHURCH AND RELIGION (1877). *Religion.*

MIXED ESSAYS (1879). *Literary and social criticism.*

IRISH ESSAYS AND OTHERS (1882). *Social and literary criticism.*

DISCOURSES IN AMERICA (1885). *Literary and social criticism.*

EDUCATION DEPARTMENT. SPECIAL REPORT ON CERTAIN POINTS CON-
NECTED WITH ELEMENTARY EDUCATION IN GERMANY, SWITZERLAND,
AND FRANCE (1886). *Education.*
Reprinted by the Education Reform League with a brief prefatory
note, 1888.

GENERAL GRANT: AN ESTIMATE, Boston (1887). *Essay.*
The two parts of this essay have not appeared as a book, or been
included in any collection of Arnold's essays, in Great Britain.

ESSAYS IN CRITICISM, Second Series (1888). *Literary criticism.*

CIVILIZATION IN THE UNITED STATES. FIRST AND LAST IMPRESSIONS,
Boston (1888). *Social criticism.*
Contains 'General Grant' and three essays on America.

REPORTS ON ELEMENTARY SCHOOLS, 1852–1882 (1889). *Education.*
Originally edited by Sir F. Sandford. Edited by F. S. Marvin, 1908.

MATTHEW ARNOLD'S NOTEBOOKS, with a Preface by the Hon. Mrs.
Wodehouse (1902). *Note-books.*
A brief selection.

ESSAYS IN CRITICISM, Third Series, Boston (1910). *Literary criticism.*
The essays on Renan and Tauler have not been collected in Great
Britain.

LETTERS OF AN OLD PLAYGOER, New York (1919). *Literary criticism.*
Edited by Brander Matthews. These letters appear in *Works* (1904),
Vol. IV.

THE NOTE-BOOKS OF MATTHEW ARNOLD, edited by H. F. Lowry,
K. Young and W. H. Dunn (1952). *Note-books.*
The literary contents of Arnold's note-books and his reading-lists.
Essential for the student.

FIVE UNCOLLECTED ESSAYS OF MATTHEW ARNOLD, edited by K. Allott,
Liverpool (1953). *Essays.*
Contains Arnold's three essays on America, an uncollected essay on
Sainte-Beuve, and 'A Liverpool Address'.

For works arranged and edited by Arnold, or containing contributions
by him, see Smart's *Bibliography*, pp. 37–42. Several essays (but none
of the first importance) are still uncollected.

Letters:

LETTERS OF MATTHEW ARNOLD, 1848–1888, edited by G. W. E. Russell,
2 vols. (1895).
Censored by Arnold's family and the editor. No index.

UNPUBLISHED LETTERS OF MATTHEW ARNOLD, edited by A. Whitridge,
New Haven (1923).

THE LETTERS OF MATTHEW ARNOLD TO ARTHUR HUGH CLOUGH, edited by
H. F. Lowry, Oxford (1932).
Contains two valuable 'Introductory Chapters'.

Many of Arnold's letters are still unpublished. Others are scattered in
books and periodicals. Students should consult 'A Check List of
Matthew Arnold's Letters' by T. Vail Motter, *Studies in Philology*,
Vol. XXXI (1934), and the article, cited earlier, by M. Mainwaring
(see under *Bibliographies*). A new check-list is projected by A. K.
Davis, Jr., of Virginia—see *The Victorian News Letter*, circulated from
Urbana, Illinois, No. 3 (April 1953).

Some Biographical and Critical Works:

THE GERM: THOUGHTS TOWARDS NATURE IN POETRY, LITERATURE, AND
ART, No. 2 (February, 1850).
Contains a review of *The Strayed Reveller* . . . by W. Rossetti.

THE POEMS AND PROSE REMAINS OF A. H. CLOUGH (1869).
Vol. I contains a review (1853) of Arnold's early poetry.

ESSAYS AND STUDIES, by A. C. Swinburne (1875).
Includes a good essay on Arnold's *New Poems* (1867).

ETHICAL STUDIES, by F. H. Bradley (1876).
Contains a merciless dissection of Arnold's religious views in a
clever parody of his style.

THE NEW REPUBLIC . . . , by W. H. Mallock (1877).
'Mr. Luke' is a satirical portrait of Arnold.

LITERARY ESSAYS, by R. H. Hutton, second edition (1877).
Includes an essay on Arnold's poetry.

THE CHOICE OF BOOKS, by F. Harrison (1886).
Contains 'Culture: A Dialogue' (1867).

MODERN HUMANISTS, by J. M. Robertson (1891).
Contains a useful study of Arnold. *Modern Humanists Reconsidered* appeared in 1927.

RES JUDICATAE, by A. Birrell (1892).
Includes a short study of Arnold.

THOMAS AND MATTHEW ARNOLD AND THEIR INFLUENCE ON ENGLISH EDUCATION, by J. G. Fitch (1897).

STUDIES OF A BIOGRAPHER, by Leslie Stephen (1898).
Vol. II contains a study of Arnold.

MATTHEW ARNOLD, by G. Saintsbury (1899).

PASSAGES IN A WANDERING LIFE, by Thomas Arnold (1900).
An important source for Matthew Arnold's early life.

THE THREE FRIENDS: A STORY OF RUGBY IN THE FORTIES, by A. G. Butler, Oxford (1900).
Contains an agreeable description of Arnold in his 'dandy' phase.

VICTORIAN PROSE MASTERS, by W. C. Brownell, New York (1901).

MATTHEW ARNOLD, by H. W. Paul (1902).
English Men of Letters series.

MATTHEW ARNOLD, by G. W. E. Russell (1904).

LIFE AND CORRESPONDENCE OF JOHN DUKE COLERIDGE, by E. H. Coleridge (1904).
Includes some interesting letters by Arnold.

MATTHEW ARNOLD AND HIS RELATION TO THE THOUGHT OF OUR TIME, by W. H. Dawson (1904).

VIEWS AND REVIEWS, by Henry James (1908).
Includes a review (1865) of *Essays in Criticism*, First Series. See also the essay by the same author in *The English Illustrated Magazine*, Vol. I (January, 1884).

MATTHEW ARNOLD ON CONTINENTAL LIFE AND LITERATURE, by A. P. Kelso, Oxford (1914).

A WRITER'S RECOLLECTIONS, by Mrs. Humphry Ward (1918).
Recollections by Arnold's niece, the author of *Robert Elsmere* (1888).

LORD BYRON: ARNOLD AND SWINBURNE, by H. J. C. Grierson (1921).
The Warton Lecture on English Poetry for the British Academy.
Reprinted in *The Background of English Literature* . . . (1934).

THE ART OF POETRY, by W. P. Ker (1923).

SOME AUTHORS, by Sir Walter Raleigh, Oxford (1923).

THE INFLUENCE OF THE CLASSICS ON THE POETRY OF MATTHEW ARNOLD,
by R. E. C. Houghton, Oxford (1923).

DISCOVERIES, by J. Middleton Murry (1924).

MATTHEW ARNOLD, by H. Kingsmill (1928).

DR. ARNOLD OF RUGBY, by A. Whitridge, New York (1928).

MATTHEW ARNOLD AND GOETHE, by J. B. Orrick (1928).
Publications of the English Goethe Society, n.s., Vol. IV.

POETRY AND THE CRITICISM OF LIFE, by H. W. Garrod, Oxford (1931).
Includes three lectures on Arnold.

MATTHEW ARNOLD, by C. H. Harvey (1931).

MATTHEW ARNOLD, by Sir Edmund Chambers (1932).
The Warton Lecture on English Poetry for the British Academy.

SELECTED ESSAYS, by T. S. Eliot (1932).
Contains 'Arnold and Pater' (1930).

THE USE OF POETRY AND THE USE OF CRITICISM, by T. S. Eliot (1933).
Contains a brilliant, unsympathetic account of Arnold.

THE SOCIAL AND POLITICAL IDEAS OF THE VICTORIAN AGE, edited by
F. J. C. Hearnshaw (1933).
Includes 'Matthew Arnold and the Educationists', a valuable essay
on Arnold's social thinking by J. Dover Wilson.

ENGLISH POETRY AND THE ENGLISH LANGUAGE, by F. W. Bateson,
Oxford (1934).
Contains some interesting remarks on Arnold's poetic diction.

STUDIES IN THE TEXT OF MATTHEW ARNOLD'S PROSE WORKS, by E. K
Brown, Paris (1935).

MATTHEW ARNOLD AND FRANCE, by I. E. Sells, Cambridge (1935).
Explores the influence of Senancour and includes an unpublished
early poem by Arnold.

REVALUATION, by F. R. Leavis (1936).
Contains a note on Arnold's poetry. See also the same critic's 'Arnold as Critic', *Scrutiny* (December 1938).

MATTHEW ARNOLD, by C. Stanley, Toronto (1938).

MATTHEW ARNOLD, by L. Trilling (1939).
A study of Arnold's ideas by a 'liberal' critic.

ON THE DICTION OF TENNYSON, BROWNING AND ARNOLD, by B. Groom, Oxford (1939).
S. P. E. Tract, No. LIII. Useful.

THE POETRY OF MATTHEW ARNOLD: A COMMENTARY, by C. B. Tinker and H. F. Lowry (1940).
Essential for the student.

KEATS AND THE VICTORIANS . . . , by G. H. Ford, New Haven (1945).
Part II is a sensitive examination of Keats's influence on Arnold.

MATTHEW ARNOLD, by E. K. Chambers, Oxford (1947).

MATTHEW ARNOLD, POÈTE, by L. Bonnerot, Paris (1947).
Scholarly and formidably detailed. An appendix contains Arnold's letters to Sainte-Beuve. There is an excellent bibliography.

MATTHEW ARNOLD. A STUDY IN CONFLICT, by E. K. Brown, Chicago (1948).
This stimulating book is mentioned in the text.

THE BURIED SELF: A BACKGROUND TO THE POEMS OF MATTHEW ARNOLD, 1848–1851, by Isobel Macdonald (1949).
Fiction, but interestingly documented.

THE EDUCATIONAL THOUGHT AND INFLUENCE OF MATTHEW ARNOLD, by W. F. Connell (1950).
A scholarly survey.

MATTHEW ARNOLD THE ETHNOLOGIST, by F. E. Faverty, Evanston (1951).

CRITICISM AND THE NINETEENTH CENTURY, by G. Tillotson (1951).
Contains three valuable essays on Arnold.

THE ALIEN VISION OF VICTORIAN POETRY, by E. D. H. Johnson, Princeton, N.J. (1952).
Contains a section on Arnold's poetry.

THE VICTORIAN SAGE: STUDIES IN ARGUMENT, by J. Holloway (1953).
Includes an interesting discussion of Arnold's techniques of persuasion.

DR. ARNOLD OF RUGBY, by N. Wymer (1953).
Makes use of much unpublished material, including an early poem by Matthew Arnold.

WRITERS AND THEIR WORK

JANE AUSTEN*: Sylvia Townsend Warner

HILAIRE BELLOC: Renée Haynes

ARNOLD BENNETT*: Frank Swinnerton

WILLIAM BLAKE*: Kathleen Raine

ELIZABETH BOWEN: Jocelyn Brooke

THE BRONTË SISTERS: Phyllis Bentley

SAMUEL BUTLER: G. D. H. Cole

BYRON*: Herbert Read

THOMAS CARLYLE*: David Gascoyne

JOYCE CARY: Walter Allen

G. K. CHESTERTON: Christopher Hollis

COLERIDGE: Kathleen Raine

R. G. COLLINGWOOD: E. W. F. Tomlin

I. COMPTON-BURNETT*: Pamela Hansford Johnson

JOSEPH CONRAD: Oliver Warner

CHARLES DICKENS: K. J. Fielding

DEFOE: J. R. Sutherland

GEORGE ELIOT*: Lettice Cooper

T. S. ELIOT*: M. C. Bradbrook

FIELDING: John Butt

E. M. FORSTER: Rex Warner

CHRISTOPHER FRY: Derek Stanford

JOHN GALSWORTHY: R. H. Mottram

THOMAS HARDY*: R. A. Scott-James

G. M. HOPKINS: Geoffrey Grigson

ALDOUS HUXLEY: Jocelyn Brooke

HENRY JAMES: Michael Swan

SAMUEL JOHNSON: S. C. Roberts

JOHN KEATS: Edmund Blunden

RUDYARD KIPLING*: Bonamy Dobrée

CHARLES LAMB: Edmund Blunden

D. H. LAWRENCE: Kenneth Young

KATHERINE MANSFIELD: Ian A. Gordon

WALTER DE LA MARE: Kenneth Hopkins

JOHN MASEFIELD*: L. A. G. Strong

SOMERSET MAUGHAM*: John Brophy

MILTON: E. M. W. Tillyard

WILLIAM MORRIS: Philip Henderson

GEORGE ORWELL: Tom Hopkinson

POPE: Ian Jack

HERBERT READ: Francis Berry

BERTRAND RUSSELL*: Alan Dorward

BERNARD SHAW*: A. C. Ward

SHAKESPEARE: C. J. Sisson

SHELLEY: Stephen Spender

SHERIDAN*: W. A. Darlington

EDITH SITWELL: John Lehmann

OSBERT SITWELL*: Roger Fulford

TOBIAS SMOLLETT*: Laurence Brander

STERNE: D. W. Jefferson

R. L. STEVENSON: G. B. Stern

SWINBURNE: H. J. C. Grierson

G. M. TREVELYAN*: J. H. Plumb

EVELYN WAUGH: Christopher Hollis

H. G. WELLS: Montgomery Belgion

OSCAR WILDE: James Laver

VIRGINIA WOOLF: Bernard Blackstone

WORDSWORTH: Helen Darbishire

W. B. YEATS: G. S. Fraser

Available at 2s. net each; starred titles 1s. 6d. net each

¶ Essays in active preparation include: *Swift* by J. Middleton Murry, and assessments of Izaak Walton, Gibbon, Wyndham Lewis, Graham Greene, C. Day Lewis and other classics and contemporaries.

WRITERS AND THEIR WORK

★

A NEW ISSUE in this series on Writers and their Work is published monthly and may be ordered from any bookseller or, in case of difficulty, direct from the Publishers, LONGMANS, GREEN & CO. LTD., 6 & 7 Clifford Street, London W.I.

Annual subscriptions (12 issues)	22s. 6d. post free
Six months' subscription (6 issues)	12s. post free
Single issues	2s. each

(Back numbers available at 1s. 6d. and 2s. each—for list of titles see inside cover.)

★

BRITISH BOOK NEWS, to which these essays form supplements, is published monthly and may be obtained from The British Council, 65 Davies Street, London W.I. In addition to an article of general or bibliographical interest, each issue contains short, informative and critical reviews, by specialists, of some 200 books. Every subject is covered, including fiction and children's books, and full details of publisher, price, size, etc., are given. Annual subscription: U.K. 24s. (or 26s.★); U.S.A. and Canada $3.50 (or $3.70★); other countries 10s. (or 12s.★).

★ With Annual Index